OLD SYDNEY
A Pictorial History

For my beautiful grandmother Agnes Anne Thomas, who passed away in 1963, and who I only knew for the first eight years of my life. Those early memories of her will always hold a special place in my heart. After losing her beloved husband from the effects of World War I, she brought her young family to Australia in the 1920s from England, and Sydney became her town.

OLD SYDNEY

A PICTORIAL HISTORY

IAN COLLIS

Contents

1 City Buildings   6
2 Sydney on the Move   24
3 People and Pastimes   44
4 Harbour and Waterways   58
5 City Streets and Parks   78
6 Construction of the Sydney Harbour Bridge   100
7 Bridge Opening   112

1 City Buildings

Sydney is rich in Georgian architecture, and much of it is directly due to the work of Governor Macquarie. He employed the services of Francis Greenway and, between 1816 and 1820, Greenway designed many public buildings in Sydney with a simple, classic beauty that has never been surpassed. Just a few of Sydney's more famous buildings that have stood the test of time and seen in this chapter are:

Customs House: Originally built in 1844, the earlier building quickly became too small for the required customs work in Sydney. The present building represents both a complete redesign and enlargement of the original structure.

General Post Office (GPO): Built over the Tank Stream, the General Post Office was constructed over 25 years from 1866 to 1891. The construction necessitated the resumption of St Martins Lane for a block between George and Pitt Streets.

Sydney Town Hall: Built in the late 1800s, the site was originally an old cemetery next to St Andrew's Cathedral, which required careful exhumation and transferal of bodies to other cemeteries. It is the only non-religious city building to retain its original function and interiors since it was built.

Queen Victoria Building: The site was used as the George Street Markets for fresh produce from 1893 to 1898. Built in American Romanesque architectural style of the period it was later slated for demolition to make way for a city car park before a restoration proposal was accepted in the early 1980s. The restored Queen Victoria Building has been described by Pierre Cardin as 'the most beautiful shopping centre in the world'.

8 CITY BUILDINGS

Queen Victoria Building about 1900. The QVB was designed by George McRae and completed in 1898. It is an example of Romanesque Revival Architecture and fills an entire city block. You can see the City Bank of Sydney in York Street. Note the fancy federation tram poles.

George Street looking south towards The Strand—a popular part of the city in the early days. Immediately to the left is the Sydney Arcade of which an identical facade is still visible on King Street. Further down near the tram is Dymocks Book Arcade and Farmers, a department store that eventually became Myer.

The Royal Hotel in George Street in 1895.

CITY BUILDINGS 11

George Street taken from Barrack St near the GPO in 1871. The building next to the post office was later demolished to make way for the Railway Ticket Office. These buildings would all eventually be demolished to make way for Martin Place.

12   CITY BUILDINGS

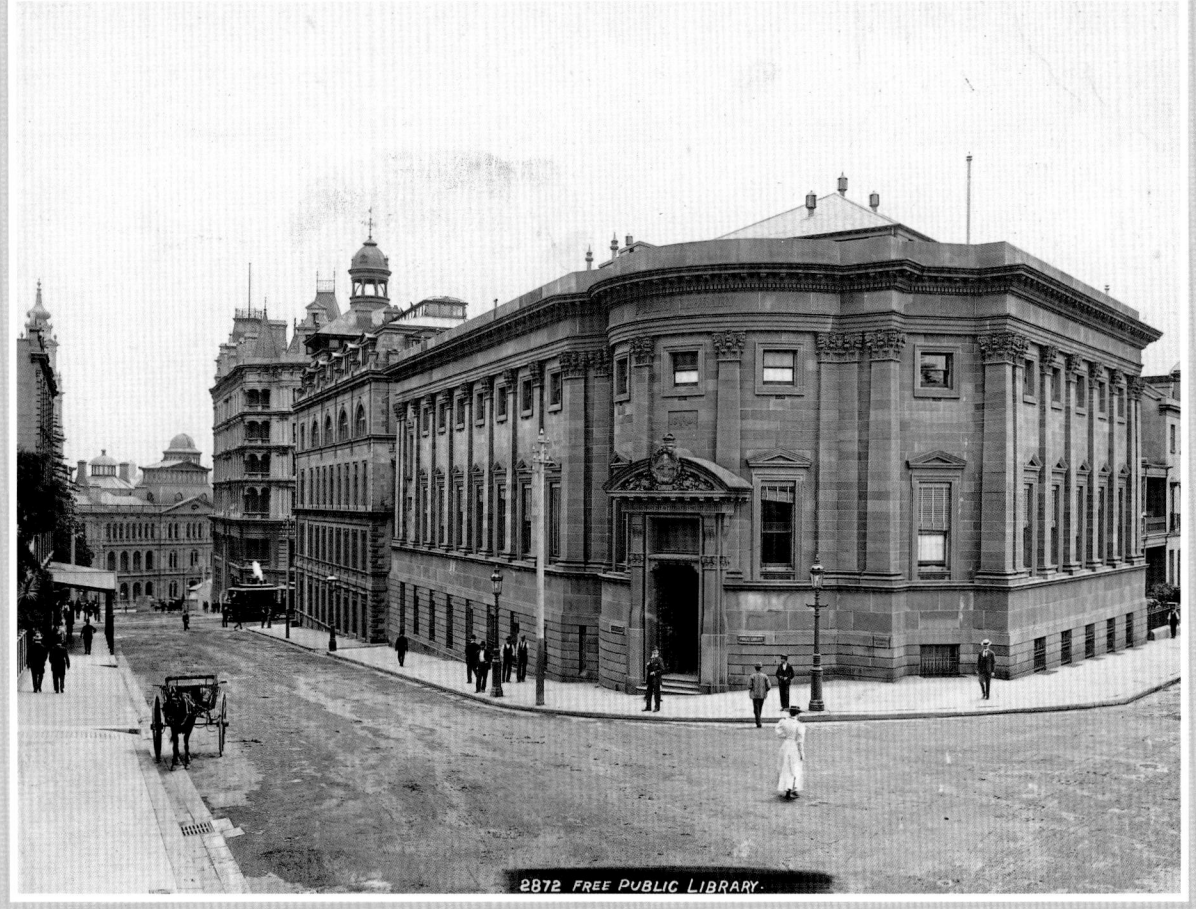

The Public Library around 1883.

CITY BUILDINGS   13

Parliament House in 1893. This building was originally part of the Sydney Rum Hospital. It was designed by Governor Lachlan Macquarie's wife and completed in 1816. At the time, colonial architect Francis Greenway commented that he thought the building was of poor design and likely to collapse. In the 1850s, a prefabricated building (originally designed as a church) was erected at the southern end and now houses the Legislative Council Chamber. Packing crates are still preserved inside the building.

14   CITY BUILDINGS

Sydney from the Lands Office, Bridge Street in 1890. Under construction is the GPO Clock, while the tower to the left is the Sydney Town Hall.

CITY BUILDINGS 15

From the Australia Hotel looking east in 1895. The church in the foreground is St James, originally designed in the 1820s by Francis Greenway for Governor Lachlan Macquarie as a courthouse, but it was converted to a church after messages from England put Governor Macquarie under pressure for "wasting money." Behind St James is Hyde Park—and another church in an early phase—St Mary's Cathedral. The Australia Hotel was Australia's first luxury hotel. Sadly, it was demolished to make way for the MLC Centre.

16 CITY BUILDINGS

The Theatre Royal in 1891. This theatre was opened in 1875 and occupies the same site in King Street today—allbeit in the more modern MLC Centre complex.

The GPO in 1892. By this time, the clock tower had been completed and it dominated the city's skyline. The demolition work in the foreground was the first phase for what would become Martin Place.

18 CITY BUILDINGS

From the GPO looking south in 1895. Seen here is Castlereagh Street, while George Street can be identified by the Town Hall Clock Tower on the right. The black area on the left is Hyde Park, while next to that you can make out the Jewish Synagogue on Elizabeth Street.

From the GPO looking north in 1895. The Quay is straight ahead, while to the right on the near shoreline you can make out Government House in the Royal Botanic Gardens.

20 CITY BUILDINGS

Wood blocking in Martin Place in 1893.

CITY BUILDINGS 21

Taken from the Australian Hotel looking west in 1893.

22 City Buildings

Corner of George and Bathurst Streets in 1898, near St Andrews Cathedral and the Town Hall. Note the front portico on the Town Hall—removed with the construction of the underground railway.

CITY BUILDINGS 23

St Mary's Cathedral looking from Hyde Park in 1890.

2 Sydney on the Move

Early transport in Sydney was by horseback, carriage or water ferry. A ferry ran up the Parramatta River from Sydney to the settlement at Parramatta from the earliest days. But these aren't the ferries we know of today. They were worked by horses on a sort of treadmill connected to paddle wheels.

The Sydney Railway Company was formed as far back as 1849. Six years later the first section of the line—from Sydney to Granville—was opened, and from then on the railway system steadily expanded. In 1926, electrification of the Sydney suburban network began, slowly replacing the old steam engines. As new railways were constructed, the coach routes were pushed back to serve more remote areas and, indeed, they played a big part in opening up new lands for settlement.

The first Sydney tramway was horse-driven from Sydney railway terminus to the city in 1862. However, as the lines stood above the road they were removed and the city remained without a tramway until 1879. In that year trams returned, drawn at first by horses and then by steam engines. They were very popular, and by the end of the century there were steam, cable and electric trams in operation, together with a large number of private horse-buses. By 1930 the increasing competition of motor-buses and private transport began to bear heavily against the trams. Gradually lines were abandoned and routes converted to bus operation.

From the beginning of steam navigation in 1831, ferrying passengers around Sydney Harbour by steam boat was the most popular means of travel. In the heyday of the ferries, before the opening of the Harbour Bridge, the biggest company operated 70 vessels. The opening of the bridge had an enormous impact on the city's commuters, with more and more people crossing the harbour in cars, trams or trains.

The wondrous age of the motor car early in the twentieth century would change the way we travelled forever. The first privately owned Sydney car was in 1906, and from those early days the motor vehicle has become easily the most popular mode of transport around Sydney.

26 Sydney on the Move

George Street in peak hour in 1902, just before the intersection with King Street. The newly completed Queen Victoria Building dominates the skyline.

Circular Quay in the 1930s. It is difficult to realise that when Captain Phillip landed here in 1788 the whole of what is now Circular Quay was covered by the waters of the cove and that the tram car on the left of the picture marks the site of the Governor's wharf.

Hansom cabs and coaches line up at Circular Quay in 1890.

Fire-fighters heading back to their fire station in Castlereagh Street in 1902.

Hansom cabs and coaches moving Sydneysiders around the city in 1890, in George Street outside the Town Hall. Note that it is before trams were introduced on George Street.

SYDNEY ON THE MOVE   31

A policeman directs traffic on the corner of George and Liverpool Streets in the 1930s. The right-hand corner remains little changed today, although the Bank of Australasia is now a bar. The Anthony Horderns side of Brickfield Hill is virtually unrecognisable with World Square now dominating the site.

32 SYDNEY ON THE MOVE

The horse ferry Bennelong pulls into Macquarie Point in the 1890s. This is on the eastern side of the present Opera House. Horse ferries provided transport between the city and North before the Sydney Harbour Bridge was built. The Manly ferry is the paddle steamer 'Brighton'.

SYDNEY ON THE MOVE

Redfern Railway Station, then the Sydney railway terminus in the 1890s. While the steam train was the popular form of travel, there were still many horse buses available for commuters.

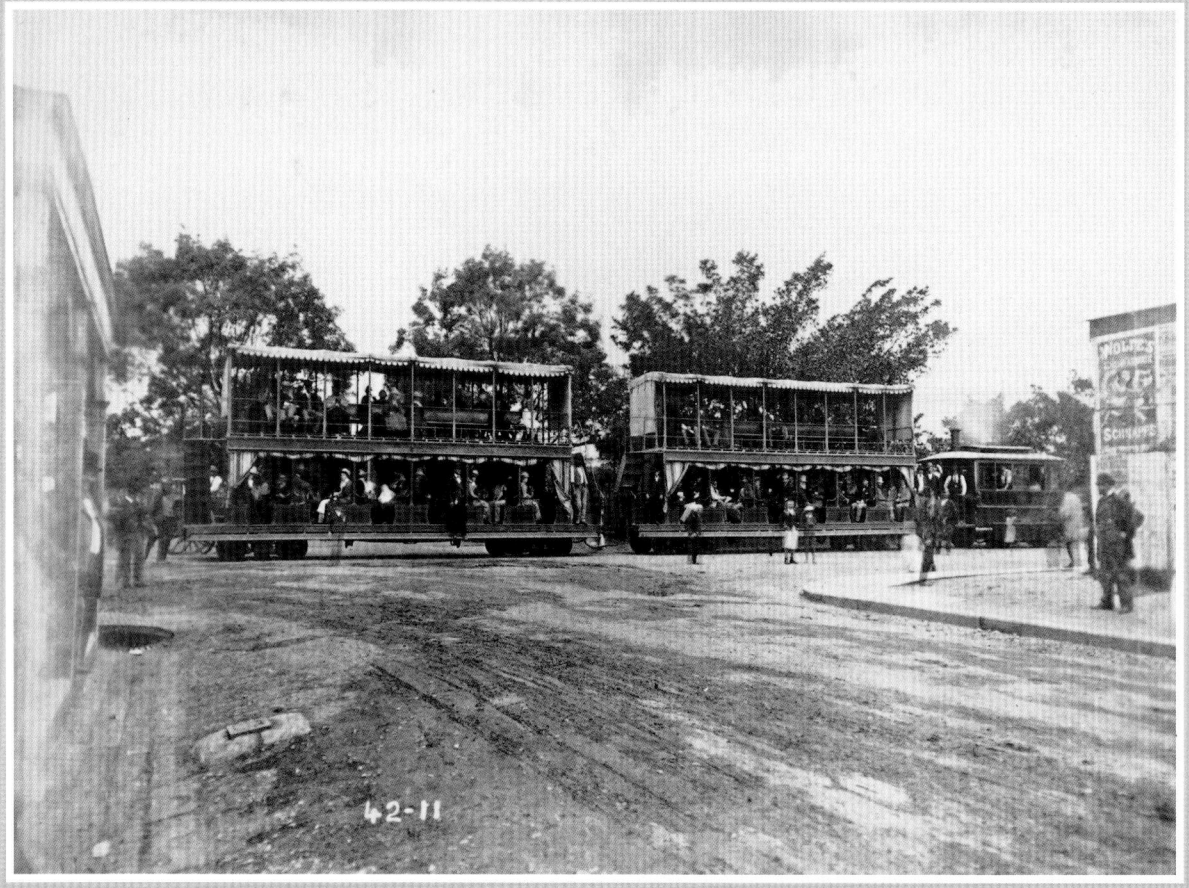

A steam tram moves through the city in the 1880s. Today a recreation of the double-storey tram, unpopular for being top heavy, is on display at Valley Heights Railway Museum.

Sydney on the Move 35

People rush to catch their means of transport at The Corso in Manly in 1900. Interestingly, both electric and steam trams can be seen in this photo.

Shoppers head into Sydney's retail stores on the corner of Liverpool and Elizabeth Streets in the 1930s. The steps are out the front of Mark Foys department store (now the Downing Centre) where it was a popular place to get your photo taken. Mark Foys was eventually absorbed by Grace Bros.

SYDNEY ON THE MOVE   37

A Sydney cable car in the early 1900s. Note the 'grip handle' to grip the moving wires in the road in the front vehicle. This line ran from King Street, Sydney, to Edgecliff.

The corner of Park and Elizabeth Streets around 1900, with the synagogue towering over the other buildings.

George Street near Martin Place in 1902. David Jones, on the corner of George and Barrack Street, is on its original site before moving head office to the corner of Elizabeth and Market Streets. Established in 1838 by David Jones, it is the world's oldest department store still trading under its original name.

An electric tram winds around the hills at The Spit, Middle Harbour.

Horses and their loads are lined up shoulder to shoulder outside the Sydney Markets in York Street. The Sydney Markets would be demolished to make way for the 'new Sydney Markets', also known as the Queen Victoria Building. The Sydney Town Hall is in the background.

Railway Square, in 1900, has horse, steam and electricity meeting head-on. Note the advertisement for department store Mark Foys on the cab, while an advertisement for department store Murray Brothers, located on the corner of Church and Macquarie Street, Parramatta, can be seen on the wall. It was affectionately known as 'Murrays'.

SYDNEY ON THE MOVE 43

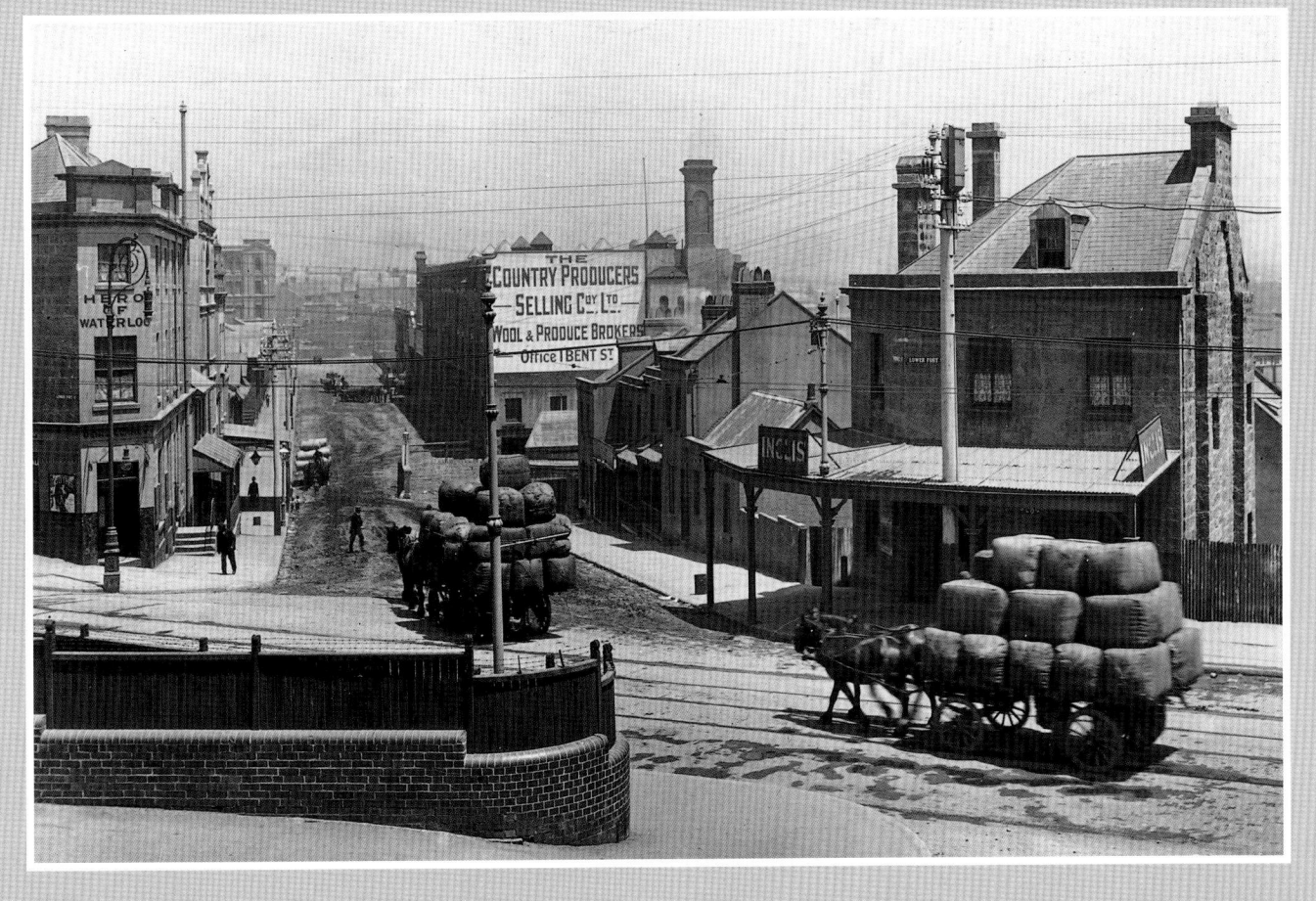

Workmen manoeuvre their loads of goods through a street of Millers Point in 1900. The Hero of Waterloo is one of Sydney's oldest hotels and is a popular icon in 'The Rocks' today.

3 People and Pastimes

Australians have always made time for enjoying their leisure activities, be it going to the beach, watching or playing sport, or simply enjoying the outdoors. Sydneysiders in particular have been spoilt for choice.

The mild climate permits indulgence in outdoor recreation, with sport high on the agenda all year round. While some games, such as football and cricket are confined to the appropriate seasons, others, such as golf, tennis and horse racing are played throughout the year.

For the not so sport conscious, the (almost) year round sunshine ensures picnics, walks, sightseeing or just lazing around are equally as popular. And with Sydney's many parks, like the Royal Botanic Gardens and Hyde Park, both situated in the heart of the city, they offer the best of both worlds.

With Sydney situated on one of the most beautiful harbours, and beaches galore within close proximity both up and down the coast, we are a water-loving city. Sailing on Sydney Harbour has always been a popular pastime, as has spending a day at the beach.

Our national pride has always been at its strongest when we have had to endure hardships. We lend a hand to the not so well-off, and turn out in numbers to farewell our brave soldiers leaving for action in far off lands. We are just as proud of our high achievers, such as Charles Kingsford Smith returning in the Southern Cross, Dame Nelly Melba making yet another comeback to the stage, or Don Bradman making cricket appear all too easy.

46   PEOPLE AND PASTIMES

A day enjoying Coogee Beach in 1895.

PEOPLE AND PASTIMES 47

1930—the fashions may have changed, but Sydneysiders' love of the sun and water remain the same.

48   People and Pastimes

Racing off Dawes Point in 1900.

PEOPLE AND PASTIMES   49

Children dressed in their Sunday best play outside a church on the North Shore, while a peddler with a horse and laden cart is ready to sell his wares.

The Bandstand in Hyde Park in 1895.

A cyclist goes for a ride in the Domain in 1890.

Pitt Street from Market Street, in the 1930s, near Her Majesty's Theatre. Her Majesty's is now part of Centrepoint while the buildings to the left housed department store Farmers. Further down were Horderns and the Strand Arcade. The Farmers building still stands and is part of the Myer Centre.

PEOPLE AND PASTIMES 53

The very popular Clifton Gardens in 1917.

54 People and Pastimes

Part of the massive crowd on 3rd March, 1885 at Circular Quay to farewell the Sudan Contingent.

PEOPLE AND PASTIMES 55

A huge crowd at Martin Place for Anzac Day in 1929. Note the cricket scoreboard on the front of 'The Sun' building. 'The Sun' was a well-read Sydney afternoon newspaper. To the right is the Commonwealth Bank, a building they based money boxes on.

George Street Markets in 1870 on the present site of the QVB. Parts of this original building were designed by colonial architect Francis Greenway.

PEOPLE AND PASTIMES   57

The very popular State Theatre, in the 1930s, often played to full houses.

4 Harbour and Waterways

Captain Arthur Phillip described Port Jackson as 'the finest harbour in the world, in which a 1000 sail of the line may ride in the most perfect security.' Few of the millions of people who came into the harbour after 1788 have had cause to disagree. Sydney Harbour has long been the source of recreation, entertainment, sport and industry for generations of people who have prospered on its shores.

The first steam mill opened at Darling Harbour in 1815, starting Australia's industrial age. Industry developed there and a giant railway yard was built.

By the 1830s, trade was thriving, and the waters in and around Sydney Cove were busy with shipping. In 1835, nearly 300 vessels reached Port Jackson from various parts of the world.

By the early 1850s secondary industries began to appear on the scene. At first they were based on local demands for such things as timber, food and clothing, but gradually they became more diverse. All the necessities of a big port and a growing city appeared—wharves and docks, schools and a university, jails, forts, government offices, newspapers, hotels and houses.

By the beginning of the 1900s Sydney was now a great port and a bustling metropolis.

Circular Quay, situated in Sydney Cove, was once an important part of the working port of Sydney Harbour and before the bridge was completed much of the population travelled to the city via the waters of the harbour. As the city has grown the harbour has become more of a haven for leisure activities, such as sailing, rowing, fishing, swimming or just enjoying the sunny conditions nearly all year round.

The harbour itself is made up of north, middle and main arms, with a total coastline of more than 300 km, and an area of 57 sq km. Spread along this lengthy coastline are fortifications, naval bases, parks, dockyards, shipping wharves, industrial and residential areas and almost virgin bushland. Navigable water is found over practically the whole of the harbour, with the deepest point off Gibraltar, on the western side of Lavender Bay, where the bottom is found at about 50 m; almost the same as the height of the Harbour Bridge roadway above the water.

Thousands of vessels pass through the heads each year from all parts of the globe. Not only is Sydney Harbour one of the world's most important harbours, but it is widely renowned as one of the most colourful, beautiful and romantic spots on the globe.

Mosman in 1880. Parts of the Old Mosman Whaling Station can be seen.

Looking across to Sydney from Blues Point on the North Shore in the 1890s.

62 HARBOUR AND WATERWAYS

A very early image of Watsons Bay, Sydney Harbour.

HARBOUR AND WATERWAYS 63

Children play in their backyard in Neutral Bay in 1910. Kirribilli can be seen across the harbour, where ferries Fairlight and Brighton are at work.

64 Harbour and Waterways

The view across to Sydney from Pyrmont in 1890. The GPO can be seen on the left, while the Pyrmont Bridge in Darling Harbour is on the right. Also visible on the right are St Andrews Cathedral and Town Hall, under construction.

Harbour and Waterways 65

The wharves at Millers Point in 1890. The Tall Ships stand side by side, with the Winchcombe Carson & Co. Wool Stores building on the far left.

Horse drawn carts are at the ready to take their goods away from Circular Quay around 1888. The site of the Museum of Contemporary Art is on the right. These stores were demolished in the 1940s and dated back to the 18th century.

Government House and the harbour from the Domain (now Royal Botanic Gardens) in 1910.

Magnificent houses already appearing at Elizabeth Bay and Potts Point in 1900.

A busy Circular Quay in 1915. In the foreground ships line up to load and unload their goods. The city skyline is already a far cry from just a few short years ago. Customs House and, behind it, luxury hotel the Metropole, face the harbour on the right.

Circular Quay in 1900, looking across at the wharves with the ferries lined up for their trips around the harbour. On top of each wharf are the ferries' destinations while on the eastern side of the quay merchants proudly display their business names. On the street, a busy city goes about its business.

Harbour and Waterways 71

Three hopeful fishermen try their luck from Fort Macquarie in 1900 (now the site of the Opera House). Note Man'o'War steps and Government House in the background..

72 HARBOUR AND WATERWAYS

Circular Quay in 1910-1915. Note there are no paddle steamer ferries, wind-jammers or ferry wharves now and the decorative tram poles on Alfred St have been removed.

HARBOUR AND WATERWAYS 73

Pyrmont looking across to Sydney in 1905, where shipping, train lines and terraces all lived together.

74 Harbour and Waterways

The ferry from the city to the north shore was the only means of crossing the harbour before the bridge was built. The image above shows people disembarking at Milsons Point in 1900, with trams also at the ready to take them to their destination.

HARBOUR AND WATERWAYS

While the Goldsbrough Mort building no longer dominates the Quay, the ever popular ferries are still getting Sydneysiders to their destinations.

Sydney Harbour and Botanic Gardens, looking from Macquarie Street, in 1900. The building on the left housed the government stables, and is now the Conservatorium of Music.

HARBOUR AND WATERWAYS 77

The Point at Mosman in the late 1800s.

5 City Streets and Parks

Perched on the edge of its splendid natural harbour, Sydney in the early 1880s was an unsightly and somewhat unsavoury seaport. It had been sprawling haphazardly from Sydney Cove almost 100 years earlier, its growth governed by profit rather than planning and concern for posterity.

The first track to be named was Pitt Street. Once it was a slumberous valley with a sparkling rivulet into which water dribbled from the slump flats of Hyde Park until heavy rain sent it charging down to Sydney Cove. Pitt Street played second fiddle to the haughtier High Street—which became George Street in 1810—perhaps because it developed in spurts until attaining its full length in the 1860s.

The heart of the city is Martin Place. Here the GPO provides one end of a measuring rod for all distances in New South Wales. It is a place of events—it became a space to congregate and communicate. It began as a laneway squeezed in at the George Street end by hoardings and shabby shop fronts on one side and the Post Office building on the other. The shops were cleared away and a wide road opened up to Pitt Street.

Hyde Park marked the outskirts of Sydney town and was dedicated for public recreation and amusement in 1810 and has maintained its original boundaries almost intact since that date. Two of the most popular national sports were practised here—horse racing and cricket. Both found keen supporters amongst the military who were garrisoned in the town.

For over a century the Domain was a place where soap-box orators would propound all types of ideas and philosophies to whoever would stop and listen.

Farm Cove, the site of Australia's first farm, was found to be poor for farming purposes. Although of little use for growing grain, Farm Cove was used for horticultural purposes. This site is now known as the Royal Botanic Gardens and is a haven for harbourside walks, picnics and botanical studies.

80 CITY STREETS AND PARKS

Bridge Street in 1884.

CITY STREETS AND PARKS   81

George Street in 1880, as a stagecoach full of passengers goes by. The Old Sydney Markets is now the Queen Victoria Building.

Looking down Market Street across Elizabeth Street in 1893 from Hyde Park.

CITY STREETS AND PARKS   83

York Street from Wynyard Square in 1888.

84 City Streets and Parks

St James Church and Queens Place in 1902, at the Hyde Park end of Macquarie Street and the top of King Street. The Queen Victoria Building and Town Hall clock tower dominate the skyline. Note the cable car passing by. The statue is of Queen Victoria.

CITY STREETS AND PARKS 85

2886. MACQUARIE STREET.
NEAR HOSPITAL.
KERRY PHOTO SYDNEY.

A horse and cart makes its way down Macquarie Street near Sydney Hospital in 1902 while the middle 'Rum Hospital' building has made way for a more substantial "Sydney Hospital". Note Parliament House on the far left.

86 CITY STREETS AND PARKS

George Street looking south in the 1890s. Note the steam trams and Sydney University on the horizon.

CITY STREETS AND PARKS   87

Elizabeth Street near Bent Street in 1902.

88 CITY STREETS AND PARKS

2891. ARGYLE CUT. KERRY. PHOTO. SYDNEY.

Workmen guide their horses through the Arygle Cut, while some youngsters gather outside the Garrison Church in the early 1900s. The picturesque arch was later entirely altered to make way for the Harbour Bridge approaches.

CITY STREETS AND PARKS   89

1449. Bridge St Sydney from Treasury. Looking W. (H King Syd)

Looking down Bridge Street from the Treasury in 1910.

Looking up George Street in the 1930s. To the left is a sign advertising the Capitol Theatre built on the site of the old Haymarkets while toast-rack trams serve George Street. This site is similar today.

CITY STREETS AND PARKS   91

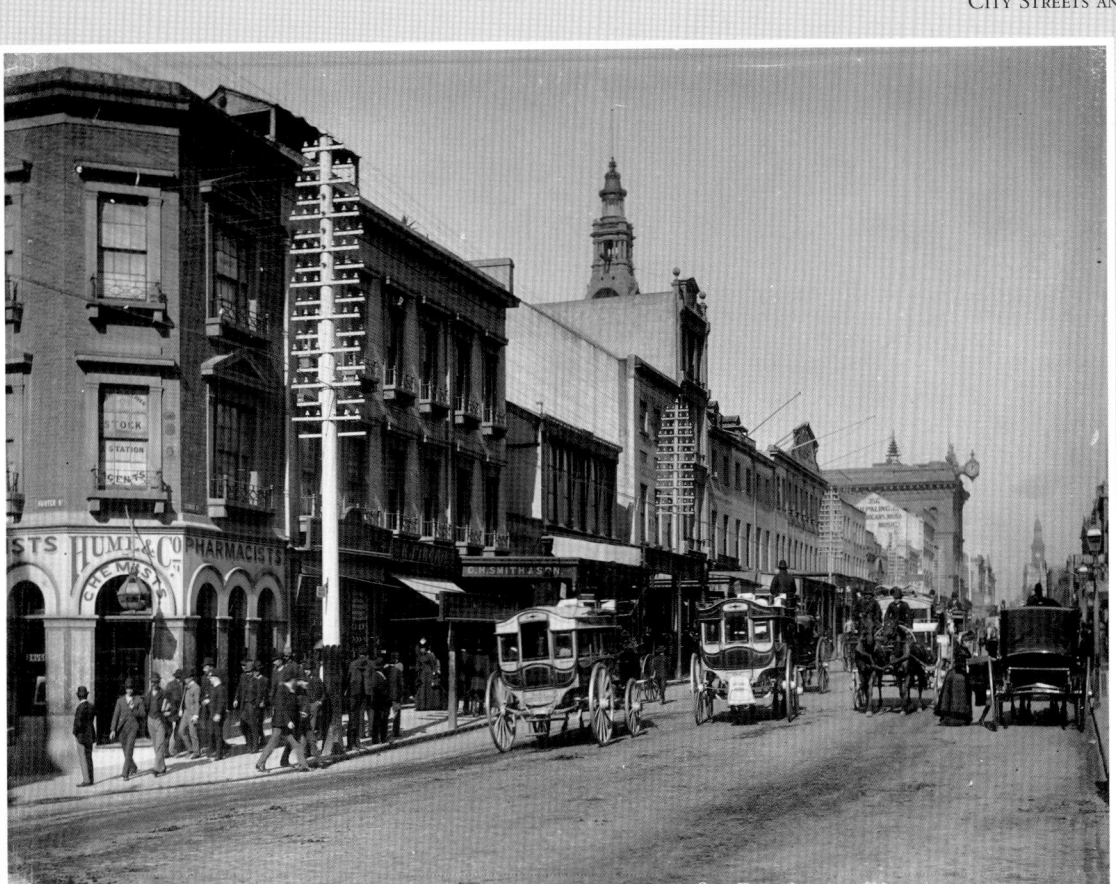

George Street near the corner of Hunter Street in 1890. Fancy carriages and bowler hats are all the rage. The Hume & Co building was built in the 1840s and still stands as one of the oldest inner-city buildings. Paling & Co, at the opposite end, would become a major music retailer. Note the GPO main clock is yet to be installed in the tower.

The corner of George and King Streets, looking towards Hunter Street in 1910. The building on the far right was once a hotel and now is the home of Darrell Lea Chocolates.

CITY STREETS AND PARKS 93

Near the corner of Pitt and King Streets in 1905. The two corner buildings still survive, allbeit with their turrets removed. The sixth building from the corner is Soul Pattisons Chemist, while the other Pitt St facades now form part of 'Skygarden'.

94　City Streets and Parks

King Street looking west in 1900. The Albert family would make their fortune from 'Boomerang' brass mouth organs and music licensing. In time, they would own radio station 2UW and a record label.

CITY STREETS AND PARKS   95

Looking down Brickfield Hill in 1910, with the magnificent Anthony Horden building on the left.

96 CITY STREETS AND PARKS

The Botanic Gardens and Farm Cove.

CITY STREETS AND PARKS 97

Sydneysiders catch a tram at the corner of Macquarie Street and Hyde Park Barracks in the early 1900s.

The Commonwealth Inauguration at Centennial Park in 1901.

CITY STREETS AND PARKS 99

Watching the Federal Poll for Federation outside The Evening News office in Sydney.

6 Construction of the Sydney Harbour Bridge

The earliest conception of a harbour bridge was that of Francis Greenway, Government Architect, in 1815 when he proposed the building of a bridge from Dawes Point to the northern shore of the harbour. It wasn't until 42 years later that a Sydney engineer, Peter Henderson, presented the first recorded drawing of a bridge designed to join the northern and southern shores. Slowly public imagination was stimulated and the bridge idea began to gain ground.

The first definite action towards building a bridge was taken in 1900 by the Minister for Works, who called for designs and tenders. Dr JJC Bradfield submitted a design in 1912 and was appointed Chief Engineer. In all, 20,000 proposals had been received. On 24 March 1924, a contract for the completion of an arch bridge was signed.

The design is a steel arch span of the two-hinged type with five steel deck truss approach spans leading to the arch on each side. The span of the arch across the harbour is 503 m; the length of the arch and approach spans is 1149 m.

Work commenced with the construction of the bridge approaches and the approach spans. While the approach spans were being built, the foundations on either side of the harbour were prepared to take the steel bearings to support the arch. On these foundations the steel bearings were set, two on each side of the harbour. Great accuracy was necessary in the placing of the four bearings, as they carry the entire weight of the arch span and its loading.

At each end of the arch span of the bridge, and just behind the bearings, a large abutment tower supports two lofty pylons. The abutment towers with their pylons are not a necessary structural feature of the bridge. They were built to enhance the appearance of the structure.

As the steelwork was erected from each shore, the two huge creeper cranes were moved from the steel ramps on top of each abutment on to the top of the arch itself. Panel by panel the cranes slowly put the steelwork into position. After it was secured, the cranes advanced outward onto the newly placed steelwork, and built out further again.

Over the central roadway portion of the bridge, pressed steel plates provided a floor on which the concrete and asphalt roadway was placed. Originally, the deck of the bridge, which is about 49 m wide, provided for a roadway 17 m wide, two footways each 3 m wide, and four railway tracks, two on each side of the bridge. A century-old dream was realised with the opening of the Sydney Harbour Bridge on 19 March 1932.

The construction of the Sydney Harbour Bridge was an engineering marvel for its time. At a cost of just over 10 million pounds, it is impossible to assess the significance of the construction and the opening of the Sydney Harbour Bridge without some understanding of the social and economic climate of the time.

102 CONSTRUCTION OF THE SYDNEY HARBOUR BRIDGE

As the vehicular ferries drop off their cargos on the North Shore, the Bridge slowly takes shape. Koondooloo would become one of the Sydney 'Showboats'. Note the ad for the Regent Theatre on the ferry on-ramp.

CONSTRUCTION OF THE SYDNEY HARBOUR BRIDGE 103

A photo taken from the vehicular harbour punt at McMahons Point, North Sydney, showing the creeper crane beginning its work from the north pylon.

104 CONSTRUCTION OF THE SYDNEY HARBOUR BRIDGE

The arches taking shape.

Workmen being transported to their workplace on top of the bridge, in a crude lift.

106 CONSTRUCTION OF THE SYDNEY HARBOUR BRIDGE

It's April 1930 and the creeper cranes are weaving the steel framework for the arch. Each crane weighed 605 tons and was able to lift 122 tons.

CONSTRUCTION OF THE SYDNEY HARBOUR BRIDGE

A famous shot of Kingsford Smith's 'Southern Sun' flying over the partly constructed bridge.

The Union Jack and the Australian flag hoisted on the tops of the creeper cranes celebrate the meeting of the lower arches and the completion of the bottom chord, as three biplanes fly overhead.

CONSTRUCTION OF THE SYDNEY HARBOUR BRIDGE   109

A deck supported by hangers, being built from beneath the centre of the arch. As the laying of the deck proceeds the creeper cranes retreat to the pylons.

110 CONSTRUCTION OF THE SYDNEY HARBOUR BRIDGE

The morning fog shrouds the bridge, which is nearly finished.

CONSTRUCTION OF THE SYDNEY HARBOUR BRIDGE   111

Miss Joan Vowell, the first woman to drive a car across Sydney Harbour Bridge September 23rd, 1931.

7 Bridge Opening

The completion of all the work was synchronised and the Bridge was opened to roadway, railway and pedestrian traffic by the then Premier of New South Wales, the Hon JT (Jack) Lang.

Against the background of the Depression, the community response to and involvement in the opening celebrations on Saturday 19th March 1932 were quite remarkable. Few other events in New South Wales before or since have achieved such participation and such publicity both within and outside the State.

The ceremony commenced at 10.00 am on the southern approach to the Bridge, opposite the Observatory. After an appropriate round of speeches, including the reading of a special message from King George V, the Premier Jack Lang officially cut the ribbon declaring the bridge opened. However, this was after Captain Francis De Groot, a former Hussar and Irishman, and a senior member of the New Guard, galloped forward on horseback and slashed the ribbon with his sword, declaring the Bridge open in the name of the 'decent citizens of NSW'.

The opening proceedings were broadcast live throughout Australia, as well as in Great Britain and America, such was the significance of the occasion. The ceremony was followed by a procession, two kilometres long, which covered a route of eight kilometres.

Aspects of our history, trade, industry and agriculture were represented in the floats. On the water was a procession of ships and boats and in the air, a display by the Royal Australian Air Force. The evening saw a Venetian Carnival on the harbour and a spectacular fireworks display. The Sydney public embraced the Bridge from the very beginning, with over one million people taking part in the celebrations.

114 BRIDGE OPENING

The official party motoring across the Bridge for the cutting of the ribbon on the north side.

BRIDGE OPENING 115

Saturday 19th March, 1932, was memorable in Sydney's history. At about 2.00 pm, after the formal opening ceremony, the bridge was opened to the public, which was thrown open to vehicle traffic at midnight.

116   Bridge Opening

A section of the water pageant as seen from Admiralty House.

BRIDGE OPENING 117

The opening ceremony moves across the bridge

The moving crowd near the southern approach, with the massive pylons an amazing sight.

As the ribbon in the centre of the Bridge was cut, aeroplanes dipped to the top of the arch in salute.

First published in Australia in 2008 by
New Holland Publishers (Australia) Pty Ltd
Sydney • Auckland • London • Cape Town

1/66 Gibbes Street Chatswood NSW 2067 Australia
218 Lake Road Northcote Auckland New Zealand
86 Edgware Road London W2 2EA United Kingdom
80 McKenzie Street Cape Town 8001 South Africa

Copyright © 2008 New Holland Publishers (Australia) Pty Ltd
Copyright © 2008 in text Ian Collis
Copyright © 2008 in images Ian Collis

All rights reserved. No part of this publication may be reproduced, stored in a retrieval system or transmitted, in any form or by any means, electronic, mechanical, photocopying, recording or otherwise, without the prior written permission of the publishers and copyright holders.

A record of this book is held at the National Library of Australia

ISBN 9781741107838

Publisher: Fiona Schultz
Publishing Manager: Lliane Clarke
Senior Editor: Joanna Tovia
Cover design: Natasha Hayles
Production Assistant: Liz Malcolm
Printer: Everbest, China

10 9 8 7 6 5 4 3 2 1